I Can See Me

By: Kinya YoungMyrie

Illustrated by: Jo Aubrey Pineda

Trilogy Christian Publishers
A Wholly Owned Subsidiary of Trinity Broadcasting Network
2442 Michelle Drive
Tustin, CA 92780

Copyright © 2022 by Kinya YoungMyrie

All rights reserved, including the right to reproduce this book or portions thereof in any form whatsoever.

Cover design by: Cornerstone Creative Solutions

For information, address Trilogy Christian Publishing
Rights Department, 2442 Michelle Drive, Tustin, Ca 92780.
Trilogy Christian Publishing/ TBN and colophon are trademarks of Trinity Broadcasting Network.

For information about special discounts for bulk purchases, please contact Trilogy Christian Publishing.

Manufactured in the United States of America

Trilogy Disclaimer: The views and content expressed in this book are those of the author and may not necessarily reflect the views and doctrine of Trilogy Christian Publishing or the Trinity Broadcasting Network.

10 9 8 7 6 5 4 3 2 1

Library of Congress Cataloging-in-Publication Data is available.

ISBN 978-1-68556-210-6 (Print Book)
ISBN 978-1-68556-211-3 (ebook)

Dedication

This book is dedicated to all the children who seek to find who they are. May you learn what God says about you at a young age and become a self-confident adult.

"Who am I?" Charlotte asked. "What do people think about me when they see me?

I imagine that I am as strong as a lion but gentle like a dove."

"Sometimes I don't believe in myself. Sometimes I'm scared and worry about what people may think," she said.

"Do people think I'm ugly or fat? Am I good enough?"

My mom told me to write down and say to myself,
"I believe in my dreams because I believe in myself."

As I close my eyes, I keep saying, "I believe in my dreams because I believe in myself.

I believe in my dreams because I believe in myself."

"I see myself as a singer."

"I see myself as an inventor."

"I see myself as an author."

"I see myself as a teacher."

"I see myself as an entrepreneur."

But when I open my eyes and see me,
I suddenly don't believe that.

I can't be all those things because I don't
believe I'm as good as everyone else.

Even though I feel like this, I must keep going. I have to change my thinking and renew my thoughts.

I have a purpose in life. I have a future and a hope. I was not born by accident.

I am fearfully and wonderfully made.

I don't have to worry about what others think, and I don't have to be afraid.

My Creator has assured me that there is no fear in love, and perfect love casts out fear.

I don't have to imagine anymore. I am as strong as a lion because

I can do all things through Him who strengthens me.

I am as gentle as a dove for I can acquire the earth.

I can see me!

I Can See Me

May you see yourself as fearfully and wonderfully made! Believe in the dreams within your heart, removing all self-doubt. Learn how God sees you at a young age as you grow into a confident adult.

About the Author

Kinya Young Myrie is an author, vocalist, actress, teacher, music therapist and owner of Treble Cakes. She resides in Baltimore, Maryland with her husband Carlton. Even as we get older, it may be hard to be confident in ourselves and conquer life without fear. We can constantly compare ourselves to others and wonder if we are good enough. Kinya's goal is to inspire children at a young age to dream big, believe in their dreams and embrace their future without fear. Kinya can be reached at www.kinyamyrie.com.

CPSIA information can be obtained
at www.ICGtesting.com
Printed in the USA
BVHW021515190722
642494BV00019B/1078